KAKAGI ICE CREAM EXPRESS

William D. Van Atta Jr.

Dedication

To my mom, dad, three brothers, and three sisters for all their loving support over the years. To the many precious furry and winged companions I have had the honor of experiencing life with.

Acknowledgment

I would like to give special thanks to my mom, who introduced me to the poems of her grandfather, Joseph Russell Taylor, and his acquaintance, Robert W. Service.

Thank you to the many teachers who patiently helped me with my deficient reading and writing skills.

For introducing me to the north woods, I would like to thank the Whiteways—Dr. Robert (Red) and his wife, Marion. I worked my way through college as the Whiteways' handyman.

About the Author

William (Bill) D. Van Atta Jr. is a veteran Army aviator and retired registered nurse who is a native of the Midwest, now living in La Crescent, Minnesota. Bill holds a Bachelor of Science degree in Geography from the University of Wisconsin–La Crosse.

After 12 years of service in the U.S. Army as both a rotary-wing and fixed-wing aviator, Bill went back to school. He graduated from The Norfolk General Hospital School of Nursing and then completed his Bachelor of Science in nursing degree at Excelsior University. He was licensed as an RN and worked in Level 1 and 2 trauma centers, where he specialized in the care of surgical, trauma, and burn patients.

When not writing, Bill enjoys spending time with his dogs. He especially likes being outdoors—camping, hiking, and photographing nature. Over the past couple of years, Bill has been putting his woodworking skills to the test by building a small sailboat. He is an avid swimmer and has competed in several open water swimming competitions.

You can connect with Bill at: running_wolf57@yahoo.com

It was a warm August day at Kakagi Lake in Ontario, Canada, and we were looking for some relief and a treat. With a treat in mind, we made our way to the boathouse and climbed aboard the small boat tied up to the dock. The boat, made of wood, appeared to be quite old. Its red hull was fading now from years of trusty use. It got its propulsion from a small Mercury outboard motor of 15 horsepower. I primed the motor, made a few pulls on the starter cord, and the motor sputtered, then fired up, engulfing us in a white cloud of exhaust smoke and the smell of gasoline.

With a gentle twist on the throttle, the boat lunged forward, and we began our journey across the lake. My sister Molly and I were on a mission. Our task was to obtain a gallon of vanilla ice cream for the hot fudge sauce I would cook up for the evening dessert. We bounced about the boat as we entered the open water, navigating our way around numerous islands and carefully avoiding the rocky hazards that lay hidden below Kakagi's waves.

After 30 minutes of wind and spray, we approached our destination. I throttled the motor back to a gentle rumble and coasted to the dock. We were now at Hanson's Hideaway Lodge. We strolled up the dock and up the hill to the lodge store. Entering the store, the squeaky screen door slammed shut behind us. At the counter, we found Ellen Hanson. We greeted each other and talked a bit, then made our way to the freezer. Molly opened the chest, reached through a frosty cloud, and pulled out a gallon of vanilla ice cream. We were on the clock now, as we had to make it back before our icy treat completely melted.

With the carton secured in a styrofoam cooler and the bill paid, we scrambled to the boat and headed back across the choppy lake. We were making good time on our ride to the Whiteways' Kakagi Wilderness Lodge, where my mom, dad, Molly, and I were guests. Our hosts were Dr. (Red) and Mrs. (Marion) Whiteway.

The lodge, within viewing distance of the lake, was accessible only by boat and had been in Mrs. Whiteway's family since the 1930s. It had become forgotten and neglected over the years until it was brought to life again in the 1960s. There was no electricity or plumbing. Water was hauled in pails from the lake, and bathing was done in Kakagi's frigid waters. It did, however, have the convenience of a propane-fueled cooking stove and refrigerator/freezer.

We left the open waters, rounded an island, and the green lodge and red boathouse came into sight. I throttled back the motor and let the wind carry us to the dock. The sound of the trailing boat wake lapped along the rocky shore, echoing through the air.

With the boat secured, we headed up the trail to the lodge with our, hopefully, still-frozen delight. We went inside to the waiting fridge and deposited the ice cream into the ice-encrusted freezer compartment. With our mission successfully completed, it was now time to make the chocolaty hot fudge sauce.

Where the recipe originated, I'm not sure. It was in my mom's recipe file on a three-by-five card that was stained with decades of spills from the recipe's ingredients. Already, I had been cooking the sauce for years, and the ingredients and cooking directions were burned into my memory. The hot fudge sauce, a mixture of butter, sugar, baker's chocolate, salt, vanilla extract, and evaporated milk, was cooked to just below boiling. As it cooked, a chocolaty aroma filled the kitchen air, pushing against the smell of the towering pine forest outside.

Tonight, it was the guests' turn to prepare the evening meal. I don't remember what my mom cooked up, as it was so many years ago. I will, however, never forget the hot fudge sauce I made and poured over the dishes filled with vanilla ice cream.

Soon the dinner bell rang, and we all gathered around the long wood table in the lodge dining room, enjoying company and the meal.

After a short break from dinner, we all took our seats again and dug into the sweet concoction placed before us. The only sound: spoons scooping up the delicious treat. With the treat complete, silence was replaced by conversation of memories past, joys of the present, and adventures waiting in the future.

Nightfall was fast approaching. The once blue sky was now painted a pinkish red. It was time—time to light the Coleman lanterns. We lit the lanterns to a chorus of crying loons. The glowing lanterns' light filled the room and flickered on the rustic walls and the moose head above the stone fireplace, bringing the old bull to life. The lanterns had a distinct hissing sound to them; it was a mesmerizing, calming sound.

Well, it was getting quite late now, and we were all tired from the day's activities. Everyone said good night, and I headed off to my room with lantern in hand. I placed my lantern on the table next to the bed and crawled between the flannel sheets. I reached over, turned the fuel knob to off, and listened to the hissing subside. The light slowly faded as the lantern burned off the remaining fuel. It was now pitch black, and I quickly fell asleep.

Even today, with so many years past, I can hear the hiss of that lantern, see the glow of its light, and taste that hot fudge over ice cream from the boat run called the Kakagi ice cream express.

Dr. William D. Van Atta Sr.

KARAGI LODGE
NESTOR FALLS
ONTARIO

9/15/80

Dear Biff —

We have decided to leave the lovely
sunset photograph here at Karagi —
eventually to be in our cabin —
Today is rainy and cold (45°) and
the picture is a beautiful reminder
of the long summer evenings —

This is the latest we have ever been
here and we certainly feel the thres-
hold of winter — as the aspen leaves
are yellowing and falling and This
years brown & dry needles cover the
ground —

Yesterday we heard & then saw
the cranes high in the sky wheeling
and organizing for their flight south —
beautiful!!

We shall think of you often as you
embark on a new phase of life —
wishing you well all the way —
Thank you for this photograph and T
two others we have — and many other
things I think you know.

Sincerely —

Marion & Dr. Whiteway

Mom (Ann), Molly (sister), and Dad (William Sr.)

KAKAGI HOT FUDGE SAUCE

½ Cup Butter

4 Squares Baking Chocolate 3 Cups Sugar

1 Can Evaporated Milk 1 Teaspoon Vanilla

½ Teaspoon Salt

Melt butter and baking chocolate in saucepan over low heat. Once melted and mixed remove from heat.

Add the sugar to the melted ingredients.

Now slowly stir in the evaporated milk and heat slowly to just about boiling.

Stir continuously to keep it from burning. While heating the sauce add salt and vanilla.

Once heated remove from burner and enjoy over your favorite ice cream.

www.ingramcontent.com/pod-product-compliance
Lightning Source LLC
Chambersburg PA
CBHW041450120626
46547CB00002B/399